· Susie Brooks ·

What's in the Picture?

Susie Brooks

What's in the Picture?

What will you find?

KINGFISHER

LONDON & NEW YORK

KINGFISHER
LONDON & NEW YORK

Copyright © Macmillan Publishers International Ltd 2019
Published in the United States by Kingfisher
120 Broadway, New York, NY 10271
Kingfisher is an imprint of Macmillan Children's Books, London
All rights reserved

Distributed in the U.S. and Canada by Macmillan,
120 Broadway, New York, NY 10271
Library of Congress Cataloging-in-Publication data has been applied for.

Illustrations: Natalia Moore (Advocate Art)
Design: Laura Hall and Suzanne Cooper
Cover Design: Laura Hall

ISBN: 978-0-7534-7530-0

Kingfisher books are available for special promotion and premiums.
For details contact: Special Markets Department, Macmillan,
120 Broadway, New York, NY 10271

For more information, please visit: www.kingfisherbooks.com
Printed in China

9 8 7 6 5 4 3 2 1
1TR/1019/WKT/UG/128MA

For Minna, with love
S.B.

Contents

What's in this picture from a tomb in ancient Egypt?

Each picture in this book has a story to tell or many different things to spot, so you'll need to use your eyes *and* your imagination!

You might find little surprises, or get a feeling from the colors or shapes. One thing is certain—the more you look, the more you will see . . .

The design was made for an important KING!

I spy with my little eye, something beginning with B . . .

The picture shows King Haremhab with Anubis, a jackal-headed god. Around them are symbols called hieroglyphs—the ancient Egyptians used these as writing. They painted messages on timb walls to help people in the next life, after they were buried.

Can you spot . . .
- **1** hare
- **2** red eyes
- **4** snakes
- **5** red discs

Find the answers at the back of the book.

How many **birds** can you see?

The King with Anubis, Tomb of Haremhab by Lancelot Crane (1910–11; original from about 1323–1295 B.C.)

LANCELOT CRANE.DELT.

What's in the kitchen, waiting to be eaten?

The table is covered in **PACKAGED** and **FRESH** foods!

Out the window, there's a view of New York City.
Can you tell which parts of this picture are painted and which are stuck on?

What belongs in the fridge?

Not my paper pancake!

Which **foods** do you recognize, and which would you like to **eat?**

Can you spot the real refrigerator door, the plastic bottles and flowers, the framed picture, and the bumpy blue wall? Wesselmann glued all these on! The foods on the table are cut out from magazine advertisments. Wesselmann painted everything else.

Still Life #30 by Tom Wesselmann (1963)

What's on the **canal** on a **sunny spring** day?

The **gold ship** is coming home after a **FESTIVAL!**

Can you spot . . .
- a red flag
- a dog on a boat
- a woman with a parasol
- a man in a white mask

It's like a postcard!

The Bacino di San Marco on Ascension Day by Canaletto (about 1733–34)

Can you find a **hat** in each of these colors: **red, orange, black, brown, and blue?**

Canaletto became famous for his lifelike paintings of Venice, a city on the coast of Italy. He often sat in a boat to sketch—but he finished his paintings indoors, where it was less wobbly!

What's at the circus show, whirling and twirling?

Costumes are SWAYING and a band is PLAYING!

I can't look down!

WOW!
The audience is spellbound by the amazing horse and acrobats. Imagine you're here in the big top, too.

How do you think you would feel?

The Circus by Georges Seurat (1890–91)

Look at the picture up close, then farther away.
Can you see the **dots?**

In this picture, the audience looks still, making the performers seem fast and exciting! Seurat painted the whole scene using lots of colored dots. They blend together right before our eyes!

Newspaper Rock petroglyphs by Native American artists (2,000 years ago)

Native American artists first drew on this rock about 2,000 years ago. Many others added to it later. They used sharp tools to scratch off the rock's dark surface. The local Navajo people call it *Tse' Hone*, which means "the rock that tells a story."

What **carvings** are **on this rock?**

They are **PICTURES** from a very **LONG** time ago!

Once upon a time . . .

Can you spot . . .
- a wheel
- footprints
- a bow and arrow
- an antelope with **3** babies

What **stories** do you think the **pictures** are telling?

What's towering over the buildings in the city?

A big **red** tower is **BURSTING** through the clouds!

It looks as if the tower is trampling on the buildings below!

Can you think of words to describe this painting to someone who hasn't seen it?

NOISY

Alive

Moving

Exciting

Dynamic

Exploding

In Paris, France, there is a tall, metal tower called the Eiffel Tower. When it was built in 1889, it was painted red. Delaunay was so amazed by this mighty, modern structure, he painted more than 30 pictures of it!

Eiffel Tower by Robert Delaunay (1911)

What's happening at the campsite and the Persian palace?

Can you spot...
- a woman washing
- a goat being milked
- **7** cups on the ground

They're both **BUSY** places where a lot of people live!

Look at all the **animals!** which can you see?

I wonder what's cooking?

Nomadic Encampment by Mir Sayyid Ali (about 1540)

He must have used tiny paintbrushes!

Can you spot...
● a man carrying firewood
● **3** musicians playing
● a sleeping cat

Which of these **homes** would you prefer to **live** in, and why?

Nighttime in a City by Mir Sayyid Ali (about 1540)

In real life, these paintings are no taller than this book, but they're packed with amazing details. They give us a glimpse of life in Persia hundreds of years ago. The people camping are nomads, who move their homes from place to place.

The Birthplace of Herbert Hoover, West Branch, Iowa by Grant Wood (1931)

Can you find any **shadows?** Where is the **sun** shining from?

This picture shows the place where Herbert Hoover was born. He grew up to be president of the United States. By the time Wood painted this scene, Hoover had moved away. The man we can see is a tour guide.

What's on this neat lawn in a country town?

We're seeing it from ABOVE, like a bird!

A man points to a **house.** Is anybody home? What **season** do you think it is here?

Don't chase the geese!

21

What's in this picture made of **squiggles** and **spots?**

It tells a SECRET STORY about **nature** and the **land.**

The **circles** might be **campsites.** What else could they be?

Can you count **4** wiggly snakes and **21** birds?

I like the wavy lines . . .

. . . I think it looks like water.

Snakes and Emus by Nym Bunduk (20th century)

Australian Aboriginal art is full of secrets about the land and the creation of the world. The Aboriginal people don't have a written language, so they use paintings and drawings like a special kind of code. The birds here are emus, found in the wild only in Australia.

Bedroom at Arles by Vincent van Gogh (1889)

This is van Gogh's own bedroom. It wasn't really crooked like this! While the soft, warm colors make the room look inviting, the thick brushstrokes and strange angles give it a restless feeling, too.

What's in the **bedroom** of a **famous artist?**

The owner has left it very **neat!**

It feels calm and cozy, but not completely ordinary!

What furniture would you have to move to open the doors?

Is the floor sloping?

The pictures look crooked!

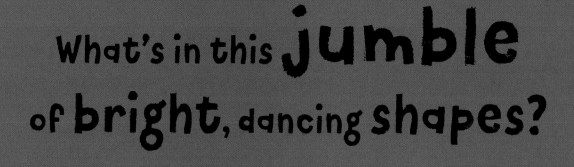

What's in this jumble of bright, dancing shapes?

Some are **SHARP**, some are **BOLD**, others are **PALE.**

Imagine you can hear the painting, just like a piece of music.

Which parts sound . . .
LOUD quiet *fast*
hⁱgh **low** s-l-o-w
happy sad?

I can hear cymbals . . .

. . . AND violins!

Composition 8 by Wassily Kandinsky (1923)

Which **instruments** do you think are **playing?**

Kandinsky likened colors to music—for example, he saw the sound of a flute as light blue. Rather than showing real things that you can touch or see, he wanted his art to make you feel something.

What's in this picture of a house in the countryside?

It's all **broken up** and **SHUFFLED** around!

Can you spot...
- **1** chimney
- **2** green trees
- **3** windows
- some orange roof tiles

I can see rain clouds.

It looks hot to me!

Landscape from Céret by Juan Gris (1913)

Is it daytime or nighttime here— or **both?**

Gris wanted to show how a place really is, not how it looks from one particular spot. He used many different viewpoints all at once, as if you're exploring the area from every angle.

Laying Down the Law by Edwin Landseer (about 1840)

In a British court, the judge wears a white wig, sort of like the poodle's fur. Landseer originally painted 12 dogs around the poodle—but when he sold the picture to the Duke of Devonshire, he added the duke's favorite English toy spaniel!

What's going on at this trial in a courtroom?

The members of the court aren't **people—they're DOGS!**

ORDER!
A poodle takes charge from his armchair.

How would you describe his character?

He looks a little snooty!

Which dogs look...
bored **excited**
suspicious happy
interested **nervous**
mischievous

Harlem Street Scene by Jacob Lawrence (1942)

Imagine you're a person in the picture.

Where are you going, and what are you doing today?

What's happening in this **bustling** neighborhood?

Some people are working, while others are having FUN!

I hope it doesn't rain!

Can you spot...

- **1** green mailbox
- **1** red flower
- **3** blue hats
- **2** yellow window shades

When Lawrence lived in this district in New York City, life could be tough, but it was always lively. He wanted to paint the everyday hustle and bustle. Look at the piano being hauled up into a building and all the people watching from the windows.

Personal Values by René Magritte (1952)

Magritte loved painting familiar things in ways that surprise or confuse us. He made ordinary objects seem strange by changing their size or putting them in unlikely places. Looking at his pictures is a little like being in a dream.

What's in this **room** with **cloudy** walls?

Are we INSIDE or OUTSIDE— or BOTH?

Maybe it's a dollhouse.

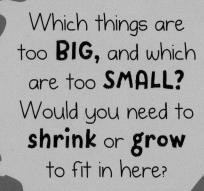

Which things are too **BIG**, and which are too **SMALL?** Would you need to **shrink** or **grow** to fit in here?

I think that's a GIANT's comb.

Bouquet of Flowers in front of a Window in Saint Bernard
by Suzanne Valadon (1926)

Imagine Valadon painting this with big dabs of thick paint. She didn't try to make it look like a photograph. The reds, oranges, and yellows are known as warm colors. They give the picture a sunny glow that soaks into the cooler blues and greens.

What's in the
window
with a sunny view?

A vase of fresh **flowers** is **blooming** bright!

Do the **colors** make you feel **warm** or **cold?**

Has someone picked the **flowers** from the **garden** outside? What are the main **colors** in the picture?

These smell lovely!

What's on the **table**, laid out for a **fabulous feast?**

The **PETS** have come to find themselves a **treat!**

A lobster lies uneaten, but someone has nibbled the pie. **Which foods can you name in the picture?**

Someone should clean that up!

Can you spot things that look . . . sharp, soft, smooth, shiny, rough, wet, fluffy?

Banquet Still Life by Adriaen van Utrecht (1644)

This picture doesn't show an actual meal! When an
artist paints an arrangement of food, musical instruments,
and other objects, it's called a still life. Van Utrecht was
excellent at painting things like this in a realistic way.

Castle and Sun by Paul Klee (1928)

Which **shapes** form the turrets, and which are the **windows** and **doors?**

Klee used colors cleverly in this painting. Can you tell how the bright yellows and greens seem closer to us than the dark reds and browns? They help us see the shape of the castle and make it look less flat.

What's in this painting of a fairy-tale castle?

A big golden SUN is shining in the sky!

Can you spot . . .
- **1** red semicircle
- **2** white diamonds
- a dark blue rectangle, an orange rectangle, and a green rectangle in a row

I wonder who lives here?

I'm building a castle!

What's at the busy waterfront, puffing out steam?

CHOO-CHOO,
look at the train!

Farewell!
Au revoir!
See you soon!

The passengers
are on board.
**Can you see them
through the windows?
Have they just
arrived, or are they
leaving?**

Locomotive along the Yokohama Waterfront by Utagawa Hiroshige III
(about 1871)

How can you tell the **ships** have come from different **countries?**

This is Japan's first railroad. It ran from Yokohama to Tokyo. In those days, many foreigners came to Yokohama by ship. Hiroshige showed both types of transportation in this colorful print.

The Old Dealer (The Old Curiosity Shop) by Charles Spencelayh (about 1925)

When this painting was first shown at an exhibition, people wanted to know where to find this antique shop. In fact, it didn't exist— Spencelayh made this scene up. Many of the things "on sale" here were his own.

What would you choose from this **shop?**

What's in the **curiosity shop,** crammed full of **treasures?**

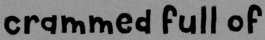

The owner is painting a **birdcage.** He doesn't have much **room!**

Can you spot . . .
- **1** yellow pitcher
- **2** clocks
- **3** empty frames
- **1** copper pan

I'd like to buy these books!

Art gallery

Here you can find out more about the paintings in this book and where you can see the original works of art. The yellow circles reveal the answers.

Lancelot Crane (English)
The King with Anubis, Tomb of Haremhab (1910–11; original from about 1323–1295 B.C.)
tempera on paper, 28. 4 x 14 in.
(63 x 35.5 cm)
Metropolitan Museum of Art, New York City, New York
This is a copy of a tomb painting made in ancient Egypt more than 3,000 years ago.

Tom Wesselmann (American)
Still Life #30 (1963)
oil, enamel, and synthetic polymer paint on board with collage & 3-D objects, 48.5 x 66 x 4 in.
(122 x 167.5 x 10 cm)
Museum of Modern Art, New York City, New York
Wesselmann loved the bright colors and shapes of everyday objects—so he used them in his art.

Giovanni Antonio Canal, known as Canaletto (Italian)
The Bacino di San Marco on Ascension Day (about 1733–34)
oil on canvas, 30.2 x 49.9 in.
(76.8 x 125.4 cm)
Royal Collection Trust, London, U.K.
Canaletto sold many of his Venice paintings to tourists as souvenirs.

Georges Seurat (French)
The Circus (1890–91)
oil on canvas, 73.2 x 59.8 in.
(186 x 152 cm)
Musée d'Orsay, Paris, France
Seurat didn't mix his paint colors—he let our eyes do that instead!

Native American artists
Newspaper Rock petroglyphs (over 2,000 years old)
etched into sandstone, 200 sq. ft. (about 19 m^2)
Newspaper Rock State Historic Monument, Utah
More than 650 designs have been made on this rock over the years.

Robert Delaunay (French)
Eiffel Tower (1911)
oil on canvas, 79.5 x 54.5 in.
(202 x 138.4 cm)
Solomon R. Guggenheim Museum, New York City, New York
Delaunay often painted views through windows. The side buildings here are curved like curtains.

Mir Sayyid Ali (Persian)
Nomadic Encampment and *Nighttime in a City* (about 1540)
opaque watercolor, gold, and silver on paper, 11.2 x 7.9 in. (28.4 x 20 cm) and 11.25 x 7.9 in. (28.6 x 20 cm)
Harvard Art Museums, Cambridge, Masachusetts
These detailed miniature pictures were made as story illustrations.

Grant Wood (American)
The Birthplace of Herbert Hoover,
West Branch, Iowa (1931)
oil on masonite, 29.6 x 39.75 in.
(75.2 x 101 cm)
Minneapolis Institute of Art, Minnesota
Hoover was born in the white cottage
to the side of the two-story house.

Nym Bunduk (Aboriginal Australian)
Snakes and Emus (20th century)
oil on plywood, dimensions unknown,
Musée des Arts d'Afrique et d'Oceanie,
Paris, France
Bunduk made many paintings on
eucalyptus bark, too.

Vincent van Gogh (Dutch)
Bedroom at Arles (1889)
oil on canvas, 29 x 36.6 in.
(73.6 x 92.3 cm)
Art Institute of Chicago, Illinois
Van Gogh painted three versions
of this picture.

Wassily Kandinsky (Russian)
Composition 8 (1923)
oil on canvas, 55.25 x 79 in.
(140 x 201 cm)
Solomon R. Guggenheim Museum,
New York City, New York
Kandinsky saw color as a keyboard of
musical notes for artists to play.

Juan Gris (Spanish)
Landscape from Céret (1913)
oil on canvas, 36.25 x 23.6 in.
(92 x 60 cm)
Moderna Museet, Stockholm, Sweden
Gris's style is known as Cubism
because of its boxy shapes.

Edwin Landseer (English)
Laying Down the Law (about 1840)
oil on canvas, 47.5 x 51.5 in.
(120.7 x 130.8 cm)
Chatsworth, Bakewell, U.K.
Landseer was fantastic at painting
animals, even when he was a child.

Jacob Lawrence (African American)
Harlem Street Scene (1942)
gouache on paper, 22.25 x 22.75 in.
(56.5 x 57.8 cm)
Private collection
When Lawrence painted this, he had
been living in Harlem, New York City,
for 12 years.

René Magritte (Belgian)
Personal Values (1952)
oil on canvas, 31.5 x 39.4 in.
(80.01 x 100.01 cm)
San Francisco Museum of Modern Art,
San Francisco, California
Magritte was a Surrealist—he loved
exploring dreams and other "beyond
real" ideas.

Marie Clémentine (Suzanne) Valadon
(French)
Bouquet of Flowers in front of a
Window in Saint Bernard (1926)
oil on canvas, 21.6 x 15 in.
(55 x 38.1 cm)
Private collection
Valadon was an artists' model as well
as being a painter herself.

Adriaen van Utrecht (Flemish)
Banquet Still Life (1644)
oil on canvas, 72.8 x 95.5 in.
(185 x 242.5 cm)
Rijksmuseum, Amsterdam,
Netherlands
Van Utrecht chose exotic fruits and
fancy tableware to create a feeling
of luxury.

Paul Klee (Swiss)
Castle and Sun (1928)
oil on canvas, 19.7 x 23.2 in.
(50 x 59 cm)
Private collection
Klee was excellent at drawing,
but he worked in a simple style.

Utagawa Hiroshige III (Japanese)
Locomotive along the Yokohama
Waterfront (about 1871)
woodblock print, ink and color on
paper, 14.4 x 29.5 in. (36.7 x 75 cm)
Arthur M. Sackler Gallery,
Washington, D.C.
This design was carved into wooden
blocks, then printed onto paper.

Charles Spencelayh (English)
The Old Dealer (*The Old Curiosity*
Shop) (about 1925)
oil on canvas, 20 x 24 in. (51 x 61 cm)
Private collection
Spencelayh trained as a miniature
artist and could paint in incredible
detail.

Index